BAREFOOT PRAISE

A Mindful Walk with God

ASHLEY CREASON

Author Photo Credit: Dayn Arnold

All other photos taken by the author and her husband

Copyright © 2017 Ashley Creason

All rights reserved.

ISBN-13: 978-0-692-99003-2

CONTENTS

Preface 4

Introduction 6

How To Use This Book 9

Ocean 12

Lake 14

River/Stream 16

Waterfall 20

Rain 22

Snow/Ice 26

Mountain 28

Trail/Path 32

Trees 34

Flowers 38

Sunrise/Sunset 40

Moon 42

Stars 46

Clouds 48

Storm 50

Birds 52

Animals 56

Wander 58

Wander 60

PREFACE

Earth's crammed with Heaven,
And every common bush afire with God;
But only he who sees, takes off his shoes.

-Elizabeth Barret Browning

I dislike wearing shoes. I understand the practicality and safety aspects of them, but I prefer being barefoot when I can. I love when my feet wander to new places, but sometimes my mind wanders too much, and I can't fully appreciate where my feet have taken me. I'm thinking about all my to do lists, or whether or not I remembered to leave the dog food and water before I left, or what I should plan for dinner when I get back home....

If our minds wander too much to the past or to the future, we can miss out on a lot of the present. This book will help you to be more intentional. To be more grounded. To be more present. To be more aware of and in awe of God. Let's take the time to savor with the senses the beauty that God created for us. Let's be mindful of the nature God created for our curiosity, pleasure, and use. Let's take the time to stop and really look, listen, smell, taste, feel, and just be in His presence. Take off your shoes and
Barefoot Praise.

Be still, and know that I am God.
-Psalm 46:10a (ESV)

INTRODUCTION

So What Is Mindfulness?

There are so many definitions of and different ways to accomplish being mindful. Basically, mindfulness is being fully aware of the present moment and all the physical, emotional, mental, and spiritual aspects of the present experience. You aren't trying to change the experience, but just to be fully in it and to notice everything about it.

There is all this cool science about how mindfulness actually fires up different parts of our brain that increase happiness and turn off the parts that feel pain. There are other health benefits, but I won't go too deeply into all of that. Just know that it is a great stress reducer, as well as being beneficial in so many other ways, and it's being more widely used within the mental health field as an aspect of therapy.

Christian Mindfulness

Even though a lot of people associate mindfulness with Buddhism and being "Zen," or think it's some hippie thing, mindfulness can be applied to and has ties to Christian spirituality as well. Jesus Himself took time to be alone to contemplate or meditate and to be with God the Father. Monks are known for similar practices. The practice of Lectio Divina, and centering and contemplative prayers, have mindfulness aspects to them. Christian mindfulness happens when we intentionally become more aware of God's presence in the moment and become more open and willing to listen to Him. Christian mindfulness helps us not to lose God in our wandering thoughts. You're not trying to empty your mind, but actually intentionally trying to fill it with Him. Christian mindfulness helps us to find God outside the walls of a church.

On the glorious splendor of your majesty, and on your wondrous works, I will meditate.
-Psalm 145:5 (ESV)

We need to find God, and he cannot be found in noise and restlessness. God is the friend of silence. See how nature – trees, flowers, grass – grows in silence; see the stars, the moon and the sun, how they move in silence.… The more we receive in silent prayer, the more we can give in our active life. We need silence to be able to touch souls. The essential thing is not what we say, but what God says to us and through us. All our words will be useless unless they come from within—words which do not give the light of Christ increase the darkness.

-Mother Teresa

How to Use This Book

Treat this like a journal or a devotional. Each page has different topics or places that you and your feet may encounter. Bible verses follow, along with space for your thoughts and observations. Explore all your senses.

What do you see? A ladybug on a branch, dew on grass…

What do you hear? Rustling of leaves, crickets…

What do you feel? Sun on your face, dirt between your toes…

What do you smell? Pine needles, sweat…

What do you taste? Salt in the air, the snack you just finished…

Be smart with touch and taste – we don't want you cutting yourself on thorns or eating sand now, do we?

Don't feel like you have to go in order. Skip around! Don't feel like your answers have to be profound or lengthy. Remember, being in the present moment means each time it is unique. Even if you were to go back to the same place twice, it would not be the exact same experience. Nature changes; you change.

Take as little or as much time as you need. If your mind starts to drift back to that to do list, or your relationship issues, or whatever else is in the past or the future, don't judge yourself. Just bring your attention back to the present moment, back to God, and the beauty He created. *Grounding* exercises, like taking your shoes off and literally connecting to and feeling the ground beneath you, can help bring you back to the present moment.

Finally, end your observations with a sort of prayer. It doesn't have to be fancy. Just give Him praise for the moment you just experienced and immersed yourself in. Nobody else was given it. You were. Nobody else gave it to you. He did. What did He reveal to you? Tell Him about it.

Now let's take off our shoes and ***Barefoot Praise***!

Ashley Creason

Barefoot Praise

OCEAN

God's Word:

Psalm 95:5

The sea is his, for he made it, and his hands formed the dry land.

Psalm 104:24-25

How many are your works, LORD! In wisdom you made them all; the earth is full of your creatures. There is the sea, vast and spacious, teeming with creatures beyond number— living things both large and small.

Psalm 148:7

Praise the LORD from the earth, you great sea creatures and all ocean depths.

What you see:

What you hear:

What you feel:

What you smell:

What you taste:

My prayer to the Creator:

LAKE

God's Word:

Psalm 104:5-9
He set the earth on its foundations; it can never be moved. You covered it with the watery depths as with a garment; the waters stood above the mountains. But at your rebuke the waters fled, at the sound of your thunder they took to flight; they flowed over the mountains, they went down into the valleys, to the place you assigned for them. You set a boundary they cannot cross; never again will they cover the earth.

Matthew 13:1
That same day Jesus went out of the house and sat by the lake.

What you see:

What you hear:

What you feel:

What you smell:

What you taste:

My prayer to the Creator:

RIVER/STREAM

God's Word:

Psalm 23:1-3a
The Lord is my shepherd, I lack nothing. He makes me lie down in green pastures, he leads me beside quiet waters, he refreshes my soul.

Psalm 98:8-9
Let the rivers clap their hands, let the mountains sing together for joy; let them sing before the Lord, for he comes to judge the earth. He will judge the world in righteousness and the peoples with equity.

What you see:

What you hear:

What you feel:

What you smell:

What you taste:

My prayer to the Creator:

Ashley Creason

> Take off your sandals, for the place where you are standing is holy ground.
> *-Exodus 3:5b*

WATERFALL

God's Word:

Psalm 147:18b
He stirs up his breezes, and the waters flow.

Psalm 104:10
He makes springs pour water into the ravines; it flows between the mountains.

Psalm 42:7-8
Deep calls to deep in the roar of your waterfalls; all your waves and breakers have swept over me. By day the Lord directs his love, at night his song is with me—a prayer to the God of my life.

What you see:

What you hear:

What you feel:

What you smell:

What you taste:

My prayer to the Creator:

RAIN

God's Word:

Deuteronomy 32:1-3
Let my teaching fall like rain and my words descend like dew, like showers on new grass, like abundant rain on tender plants. I will proclaim the name of the LORD. Oh, praise the greatness of our God!

Genesis 9:16
Whenever the rainbow appears in the clouds, I will see it and remember the everlasting covenant between God and all living creatures of every kind on the earth.

What you see:

What you hear:

What you feel:

What you smell:

What you taste:

My prayer to the Creator:

Ashley Creason

Barefoot Praise

SNOW/ICE

God's Word:

Psalm 147:16
He spreads the snow like wool and scatters the frost like ashes.

Job 37:5-7, 10
God's voice thunders in marvelous ways; he does great things beyond our understanding. He says to the snow, "Fall on the earth," and to the rain shower, "Be a mighty downpour." So that everyone he has made may know his work. The breath of God produces ice, and the broad waters become frozen.

What you see:

What you hear:

What you feel:

What you smell:

What you taste:

My prayer to the Creator:

MOUNTAIN

God's Word:

Psalm 95:4

In his hand are the depths of the earth, and the mountain peaks belong to him.

Psalm 90:1-2

Lord, you have been our dwelling place throughout all generations. Before the mountains were born or you brought forth the whole world, from everlasting to everlasting you are God.

Psalm 121:1-2

I lift up my eyes to the mountains—where does my help come from? My help comes from the Lord, the Maker of heaven and earth.

What you see:

What you hear:

What you feel:

What you smell:

What you taste:

My prayer to the Creator:

Ashley Creason

Barefoot Praise

TRAIL/PATH

God's Word:

Psalm 23:3b
He guides me along the right paths for his name's sake.

Psalm 119:105
Your word is a lamp for my feet, a light on my path.

Psalm 16:11
You make known to me the path of life; you will fill me with joy in your presence, with eternal pleasures at your right hand.

Proverbs 4:26
Give careful thought to the paths for your feet and be steadfast in all your ways.

What you see:

What you hear:

What you feel:

What you smell:

What you taste:

My prayer to the Creator:

TREES

God's Word:

Psalm 96:12
Let the fields be jubilant, and everything in them; let all the trees of the forest sing for joy.

Psalm 1:1-3
Blessed is the one who does not walk in step with the wicked or stand in the way that sinners take or sit in the company of mockers, but whose delight is in the law of the Lord, and who meditates on his law day and night. That person is like a tree planted by streams of water, which yields its fruit in season and whose leaf does not wither—whatever they do prospers.

What you see:

What you hear:

What you feel:

What you smell:

What you taste:

My prayer to the Creator:

Ashley Creason

Barefoot Praise

FLOWERS

God's Word:

Matthew 6:28-30
And why do you worry about clothes? See how the flowers of the field grow. They do not labor or spin. Yet I tell you that not even Solomon in all his splendor was dressed like one of these. If that is how God clothes the grass of the field, which is here today and tomorrow is thrown into the fire, will he not much more clothe you—you of little faith?

Psalm 40:8
The grass withers, the flower fades, but the word of our God will stand forever.

What you see:

What you hear:

What you feel:

What you smell:

What you taste:

My prayer to the Creator:

SUNRISE/SUNSET

God's Word:

Psalm 19:1-2, 6
The heavens declare the glory of God; the skies proclaim the work of his hands. Day after day they pour forth speech; night after night they reveal knowledge. It rises at one end of the heavens and makes its circuit to the other; nothing is deprived of its warmth.

Psalm 113:3
From the rising of the sun to the place where it sets, the name of the LORD is to be praised.

What you see:

What you hear:

What you feel:

What you smell:

What you taste:

My prayer to the Creator:

MOON

God's Word:

Psalm 104:19
He made the moon to mark the seasons, and the sun knows when to go down. You bring darkness, it becomes night, and all the beasts of the forest prowl.

Psalm 8:3-4
When I consider your heavens, the work of your fingers, the moon and the stars, which you have set in place, what is mankind that you are mindful of them, human beings that you care for them?

What you see:

What you hear:

What you feel:

What you smell:

What you taste:

My prayer to the Creator:

Ashley Creason

Done properly, the spiritual practice of going barefoot can take you halfway around the world and wake you up to your own place in the world all at the same time. It can lead you to love God with your whole self, and your neighbor as yourself, without leaving your backyard. Just do it, and the doing will teach you what you need to live.... You have everything you need to ground yourself in God.

Prayer ... is waking up to the presence of God no matter where I am or what I am doing. When I am fully alert to whatever or whoever is right in front of me; when I am electrically aware of the tremendous gift of being alive; when I am able to give myself wholly to the moment I am in, then I am in prayer. Prayer is happening, and it is not necessarily something that I am doing. God is happening, and I am lucky enough to know that I am in The Midst.

-Barbara Brown Taylor in *An Altar in the World*

STARS

God's Word:

Psalm 147:4

He determines the number of the stars and calls them each by name.

I Corinthians 15:40-41

There are also heavenly bodies and there are earthly bodies; but the splendor of the heavenly bodies is one kind, and the splendor of the earthly bodies is another. The sun has one kind of splendor, the moon another and the stars another; and star differs from star in splendor.

What you see:

What you hear:

What you feel:

What you smell:

What you taste:

My prayer to the Creator:

CLOUDS

God's Word:

Psalm 19:1-7
The heavens declare the glory of God; the skies proclaim the work of his hands.

Psalm 147:8
He covers the sky with clouds; he supplies the earth with rain and makes grass grow on the hills.

Psalm 104:3b
He makes the clouds his chariot and rides on the wings of the wind.

What you see:

What you hear:

What you feel:

What you smell:

What you taste:

My prayer to the Creator:

STORM

God's Word:

Job 37:14b-15
Stop and consider God's wonders. Do you know how God controls the clouds and makes his lightning flash?

Matthew 24:27
For as lightning that comes from the east is visible even in the west, so will be the coming of the Son of Man.

What you see:

What you hear:

What you feel:

What you smell:

What you taste:

My prayer to the Creator:

BIRDS

God's Word:

Matthew 6:26-27
Look at the birds of the air; they do not sow or reap or store away in barns, and yet your heavenly Father feeds them. Are you not much more valuable than they? Can any one of you by worrying add a single hour to your life?

Psalm 50:11
I know every bird in the mountains, and the insects in the fields are mine.

What you see:

What you hear:

What you feel:

What you smell:

What you taste:

My prayer to the Creator:

Ashley Creason

ANIMALS

God's Word:

Job 12:7-10
But ask the animals, and they will teach you, or the birds in the sky, and they will tell you; or speak to the earth, and it will teach you, or let the fish in the sea inform you. Which of all these does not know that the hand of the LORD has done this? In his hand is the life of every creature and the breath of all mankind.

Psalm 104:24, 27-28
How many are your works, LORD! In wisdom you made them all; the earth is full of your creatures. All creatures look to you to give them their food at the proper time. When you give it to them, they gather it up, when you open your hand, they are satisfied with good things.

What you see:

What you hear:

What you feel:

What you smell:

What you taste:

My prayer to the Creator:

WANDER

God's Word:

Romans 1:20-21, 25

For since the creation of the world God's invisible qualities—his eternal power and divine nature—have been clearly seen, being understood from what has been made, so that people are without excuse. For although they knew God, they neither glorified him as God nor gave thanks to him, but their thinking became futile and their foolish hearts were darkened. They exchanged the truth about God for a lie, and worshiped and served created things rather than the Creator—who is forever praised. Amen.

Psalm 104:33-34

I will sing to the Lord all my life; I will sing praise to my God as long as I live. May my meditation be pleasing to him, as I rejoice in the Lord.

What you see:

What you hear:

What you feel:

What you smell:

What you taste:

My prayer to the Creator:

Ashley Creason

WANDER

God's Word:

Psalm 148:3-13
Praise him, sun and moon; praise him, all you shining stars. Praise him, you highest heavens and you waters above the skies. Let them praise the name of the Lord, for at his command they were created, and he established them for ever and ever—he issued a decree that will never pass away. Praise the Lord from the earth, you great sea creatures and all ocean depths, lightning and hail, snow and clouds, stormy winds that do his bidding, you mountains and all hills, fruit trees and all cedars, wild animals and all cattle, small creatures and flying birds, kings of the earth and all nations, you princes and all rulers on earth, young men and women, old men and children. Let them praise the name of the Lord, for his name alone is exalted; his splendor is above the earth and the heavens.

What you see:

What you hear:

What you feel:

What you smell:

What you taste:

My prayer to the Creator:

www.ingramcontent.com/pod-product-compliance
Lightning Source LLC
LaVergne TN
LVHW010035070426
835507LV00006B/141